AROUND
THE WELLAND VALLEY
IN OLD PHOTOGRAPHS

COLLECTED BY
STEPH MASTORIS

ALAN SUTTON

LEICESTERSHIRE MUSEUMS, ARTS AND RECORDS SERVICE.

Alan Sutton Publishing Limited
Phoenix Mill · Far Thrupp · Stroud · Gloucestershire

in association with
LEICESTERSHIRE MUSEUMS, ARTS & RECORDS SERVICE

First published 1991

British Library Cataloguing in Publication Data

The Welland Valley in old photographs.
I. Mastoris, S. N. (Stephanos N)
942.544

ISBN 0-86299-977-4

Front Cover Illustration:
MARKET DAY AT MARKET HARBOROUGH, the Square, 1890s. Livestock, produce and goods from the Welland Valley villages and farms are on sale, while local gossip is exchanged. One of a series of photographs of market and fair days at Harborough taken by Gulliver Speight from the window of his studio on the south side of the Square.

Typeset in 9/10 Korinna.
Typesetting and origination by
Alan Sutton Publishing Limited.
Printed in Great Britain by
The Bath Press, Avon.

CONTENTS

THE PHOTOGRAPHER PHOTOGRAPHED in the Square, Market Harborough, late 1900s. He is snapped while recording a flooding River Welland. As usual there are plenty of children on hand to advise and be recorded for posterity.

INTRODUCTION

This book looks at the topography, economy, life and tradition of the upper part of the Welland Valley through the eyes of many photographers working during the last hundred years.

The pictures are divided into four sections, each dealing with one of these themes, and the prefaces to them explain a little more of what is shown. In general, this book has been designed to complement the earlier *Around Market Harborough in Old Photographs*. Where that book dealt to a large extent with the town and its industries, this volume concentrates on the surrounding villages and local agriculture and rural trades. Both books try to tell the story of people and their interaction with the local places and events, but this volume examines community life more extensively.

The area covered by these photographs straddles the first thirty miles of the Welland river valley, extending from Naseby and Husbands Bosworth in the west to Great Easton and Rockingham in the east, and from Kibworth in the north to Kelmarsh in the south. This border country — part in Leicestershire and part in Northamptonshire — has formed a discrete economic and social entity for centuries. This is due largely to the influence of the widespread pastoral agriculture practised here until the 1940s and of Market Harborough, the only sizable town which lies at the heart of the area.

Most of the photographs which make up this book form part of the collection of the Harborough Museum, a branch of the Leicestershire Museums, Arts and Records Service. Although the museum began life in 1982 with a good collection of historic photographs accumulated by the local historical society, the past few years have seen extensive additions to its holdings. Many of these have been donated, but even more have been actively sought by staff from personal family collections and copied while on short term loan to the museum.

The images reproduced here come from three types of photographer. The first is the pure amateur whose interest in reportage or the art of photography has often led to remarkable work. The work of the Revd William Law and Bernard Elliott is typical of these. Law was active between the 1840s and the 1890s, a period which saw the birth and rapid maturity of the science of photography. Much of his work reflects this with examples of daguerreotypes, calotypes and wet collodion images, as well as many repetitive scenes taken as tests for different materials and techniques. Elliott, on the other hand, was working from the 1920s to the 1950s and was much more concerned with recording places and events on his standard format roll film. His work as Sanitary Inspector for Market Harborough Urban District Council provided him with many opportunities to use his photographic skill to record the growth of the modern town and the demolition of many older buildings in the area. The section dealing with public amenities owes much to Elliott's work.

The second type of photographer represented here is the press and commercial professional. This work is easily recognizable for its technical quality and rather stagey composition. The best known topographical work of this type was produced by the Webb brothers of Market Harborough, who ran their commercial photographic processing and postcard business from the 1920s to the 1960s.

The third type of photographer is a hybrid of the other two. A handful of exceptionally talented village postmasters were also keen amateur photographers. They saw the commercial opportunities offered by the 'postcard mania' of early this century and supplied it by creating their own local picture postcards. Their products provide a fascinating and unique record of people, places and events in their own and surrounding villages. The two most important postmaster photographers in the Welland Valley were Endor Halford of Naseby (active 1900s to 1930s) and Frederick Hawke of Hallaton (active 1900s to 1930s). The sections on topography and ceremonies are greatly indebted to their work.

Viewing images of past life is an emotive experience which often engenders a frustration with the present. It is hoped that the interpretation offered of these photographs will diffuse such nostalgia. Many details have been culled from oral reminiscences by senior members of the village communities, and this information suggests that much of the change recorded here has definitely been for the better. The large number of photographs of the past century should not blind us into thinking earlier times an idyll, unchanging and lacking social or economic problems. Change is the very process of history and we should be grateful that, unlike earlier social revolutions, photography has been available to record at least some of the making of modern life.

* * *

As archival negatives exist for most of the photographs reproduced here, readers may easily order copies for their own use from the Harborough Musuem. The museum is always keen to acquire or copy other historic photographs of the Welland Valley area.

SECTION ONE

Around the Valley

This section looks at the buildings, landscape and landmarks of the Welland Valley.

Many of the photographs show the extensive changes which have taken place throughout the area, but this should not really surprise us, considering the rapid developments which have occurred in agriculture, industry, transportation and general living standards within the past century. In fact it is a considerable testimony to the valley's character that so many of its places retain such a strong sense of individuality today.

The photographs are organized in the form of four circular tours: west, east, north and south from Market Harborough.

AERIAL VIEW OF MARKET HARBOROUGH, 1926. Looking east across the town, St Mary's Road can be seen at the top of the photograph, with the High Street running to the left and Northampton Road to the right. Coventry Road and Nelson Street are converging as they approach the bottom of the picture. The first major phase of suburban developments can be seen clearly here. On the bottom left lies New Harborough (see p. 12), while at the top left can be seen Clarence Street and its extension as The Broadway (p. 30). As yet, Roman Way and the Bowden Fields Estate (p. 121) have not been built, nor the Welland Park and Southern Estates (pp. 29, 51 & 124).

MARKET DAY ON THE SQUARE, Market Harborough, 1902. The market has always lain at the heart of life in Market Harborough. Indeed, the town's origins arise from the creation of a planned marketing centre to serve the Welland Valley. Weekly sales of livestock and produce have been held here every Tuesday since the 1220s. This photograph was taken just before the livestock market was relocated to a purpose built site on Springfield Street (see p. 58).

HIGH STREET, Market Harborough, c. 1910. As well as its market, the town has benefited from being situated on the A6. In the 17th and 18th centuries the volume of road traffic helped develop a number of large inns along the High Street, the most famous being the Three Swans. The early motor car and Stevens' garage seen here presage the revival of this trade which had been seriously diminished by the arrival of the railway to the town in the 1850s.

NELSON STREET, Market Harborough, c. 1910. The built-up area of Market Harborough did not increase until the middle of the 19th century and then the first real initiative came from the town's Freehold Land Society. The Society's first estate began here, either side of the eastern end of Nelson Street, in the 1870s.

NELSON STREET, Market Harborough, c. 1910. The main stretch of Nelson Street formed the southern boundary of the Freehold Land Society's third (and most important) estate. Developed from the 1880s, the area was originally to be called the 'Victoria Estate', but the more colloquial (and correct) 'New Harborough' was soon favoured. George Gardiner, who kept the shop and post office seen here was the local agent and first Secretary of the Freehold Land Society.

Logan Street Recreation Grounds, Market Harborough.

LOGAN STREET RECREATION GROUND, Market Harborough, c. 1910. This was the first planned civic amenity in New Harborough and was created through the generosity of the local MP, J. W. Logan. In 1895 he purchased the land and gave it to the town council to be laid out as a recreation space. In 1906 a further portion was added, donated by the Town Feoffees.

WORKERS LEAVING HEARTH'S FACTORY, Logan Street, Market Harborough, c. 1914. The Freehold Land Society was not content to facilitate members in purchasing land to build homes, but actively sought to attract new employment to its estates. In the early 1890s it enticed the Leicester-based hosiery firm of Hearth & Co. to open a factory in Logan Street and build nineteen houses in Hearth Street to house the workers. In 1892 Hobson & Son (shoe makers) built a factory in Highfield Street.

MAIN STREET, Lubenham, c. 1860. Here the three most important secular buildings in the village form one compact row. In the centre of the picture is the Swan Inn which had been built in 1700. It was extensively rebuilt in the early 1870s and renamed the Coach and Horses. To the right is a house and one-storey shop kept by the Collins family, who worked as grocers and shoemakers and also kept the post office. The next building, partially hidden by the carrier's cart, was the village bakehouse.

THE VILLAGE POND, Lubenham, 1910s. The wall around this pond, known locally as the 'town pit', was built in 1869. In 1949 the pond was filled in and a war memorial erected on the site (see p. 139).

(see p. 139).

TOWER HOUSE, Lubenham, 1910s. Originally known as 'the Cottage', this house was rebuilt in the 1860s by B.J. 'Cherry' Angell, a local racing enthusiast. He owned the first two winners of the Grand National Hunt Steeplechase, which was originally run at Lubenham in 1860. In 1866 he helped to set up the National Hunt Committee.

PAPILLON HALL, Lubenham, September 1944. This country house on the western outskirts of the village took its name from David Papillon, a Royal Fortifications engineer (d. 1659). It was rebuilt in 1902 by Edwin Lutyens but fell into disuse after military occupation during World War Two. It was finally demolished in 1950.

AMERICAN SERVICEMEN AT PAPILLON HALL, September 1944. Perhaps the most well-known military occupants of the hall were members of the 82nd Airborne Division of the US Army. Here John D. Gutshall, Charles L. Sartain and Marvin L. Ragland of the 319th Glider Field Artillery Battalion pose for a photograph in front of the house lily pond, just before leaving for Nijmegen.

THE STABLE BLOCK at Papillon Hall, September 1944. The 319th Battalion was billeted at the Hall from February to September 1944. Six men occupied each stall in the stables.

THE ROSE COTTAGE TEA ROOM, Main Street, Foxton, 1920s. The nearby canal and flight of locks (see p. 49) have brought many visitors to the village since the 19th century.

CORONATION CELEBRATIONS at Gumley Hall, 1911. Here villagers from Gumley and the surrounding farms celebrate the coronation of George V on the lawn in front of Gumley Hall. The marquee has been supplied by Lynn's of Kibworth (see p. 46). The hall was built in 1764, with additions in the 1860s. During World War Two it was the base for 'Special Training Squad No.4', where resistance fighters from occupied countries were trained.

MAIN STREET, Theddingworth, c. 1910. Looking west.

HIGH STREET, Husbands Bosworth, c. 1880.

BOSWORTH HALL, Husbands Bosworth, 1920s. This complex building has a mediaeval core surrounded by 16th- and 17th-century wings 'tudorized' in the 19th century. Beyond is the east wing which is a classical range of buildings designed by Joseph Bonomi in 1792. The hall served as a Roman Catholic mass centre from 1630 until a church was built in the grounds in 1873.

CHURCH LANE, Husbands Bosworth, c. 1920. This used to be known locally as Gilby's Lane, after a family of plumbers and decorators who lived there.

THE CANAL TUNNEL, Kilworth end, Husbands Bosworth, 1910. This portion of the Grand Union Canal was constructed in 1813. The terrain required cutting this 1,000 yard tunnel with a horse depot at the eastern end and a coal wharf at the Kilworth end. Boats had to be 'legged' through by their crew, as there was no walkway for draught horses.

SULBY HALL, Sulby, C. 1914. The hall was built in 1792 to designs of Sir John Soane. Like many other mansions in the Welland Valley it fell on hard times after World War Two. It was demolished in 1948.

Source of River Nen, Naseby.

SOURCE OF THE RIVER NENE, Naseby, C. 1910. Until the middle of this century Naseby was credited with being the source of three rivers: the Avon, the Welland and the Nene. However this rather inauspicious beginning for Northamptonshire's greatest river is now considered to be a tributary of the main source which rises near Daventry. The spring is located about a mile to the south of Naseby, on the Thornby Road.

THE BELL INN, Naseby, 1880s. This inn stood on the site of the present car park to the Fitzgerald Arms, whose gable can be seen behind the right-hand portion of the roof.

GYNWELL, Naseby, C. 1900. At this time the farmhouse and barn were owned by the Wilford family, who were both small-holders and the village carriers. The walls of the barn are made from cob – mud mixed with straw and small stones. These required stone foundations and a well thatched roof to preserve them. The buildings were demolished in the mid-1950s.

THE ROUND HOUSE AND FROG'S ROW, Naseby, 1900s. The Round House was probably built in the 17th century as a dovecote. In the 1920s the roof was blown off and it became derelict. Frog's Row was also known as Wilford's Yard or Chapel Row. It was demolished in 1938.

TITHE BARN, Church Street, Naseby, c. 1910. This fine timber-framed barn was built in 1651 by Edward Shuckburgh, a major landowner in the village who lived opposite in Shuckburgh House. Despite being restored in 1908 and 1931, the barn was demolished in 1950.

THE NASEBY 'OLD MAN', when at Maidwell Hall, 1913. This large hollow copper ball is now on display in Naseby parish church. It originally came to England as booty after the Battle of Boulogne Harbour in 1544 and adorned Horseheath Hall, Cambs. until 1790. Then it was used to crown the truncated spire of Naseby church and acquired the nickname 'Old Man'. In 1860 it was taken down and between 1888 and 1934 it was used as a garden ornament at Maidwell Hall.

COMMEMORATIVE OBELISK FOR THE BATTLE OF NASEBY, Naseby, c. 1910. On the 14 June 1645, Royalist and Parliamentary forces met at Naseby and fought one of the major battles of the English Civil War in the fields to the north of the village, between the Clipston and Sibbertoft roads. This monument was erected in 1823 by Mary and John Fitzgerald on the site of a windmill which had burnt down in the 18th century. It was not meant to mark a specific part of the battlefield.

THE CROMWELL LIBRARY, School Lane , Naseby, c. 1910. A village reading-room and library was established in the central portion of this building in 1884, along with a surgery for visiting doctors from Welford and Guilsborough. However in 1899 an appeal was launched to create a library devoted to the Civil War and in 1901 the Cromwell Memorial Library was opened. Around 1919 the books were moved to the school and in the 1950s to the new village hall, where they still remain.

Cromwell Library, Naseby

HIGH STREET, Clipston, 1950s. Clipston Grammar School is on the right and next to it are the almshouses built in 1928 to replace those formerly in the school (see pp. 96 & 140).

THE HARBOROUGH ROAD, Clipston, c. 1900. On the left is the Bull's Head pub and beyond it The Green.

GOLD STREET, Clipston, c. 1900. The origin of the name Gold Street is unknown. The thatched row of cottages on the left was later replaced by a branch of the Market Harborough Co-Op.

KING CHARLES'S OAK TREE, Sibbertoft, 1900s. This oak tree stood to the north of the road between Sibbertoft and Naseby and was one of many locations in the neighbourhood of Naseby Battlefield which local tradition says sheltered Charles I. The tree was destroyed by fire in the 1950s.

CHURCH STREET, C. 1875. The River Welland rises from a spring on the west side of the village, and after running west and north for a little, it turns east near Husbands Bosworth sand pit and then begins its long journey to the Wash.

MARSTON TRUSSELL HALL, C. 1900. This mansion was an almost total rebuild in the 1840s of a Tudor residence. In the foreground is William Ewins Bennett, the owner and local squire.

MAIN STREET, Marston Trussell, 1950s. Looking east to the junction with the Sibbertoft Road.

WELLAND PARK, Market Harborough, 1940s. Welland Park was created in 1932 as part of a large council development of the town to the south of the river. This not only included private and council housing but also a school and a major road designed as a bypass for the town.

THE RIVER WELLAND at Market Harborough, 1920s. Looking east down stream to a foot bridge which was first built in the early 19th century.

CLARENCE STREET, Market Harborough, c. 1910. This street was the only result of an ambitious estate planned in the early 1890s, which was to have occupied a former brickfield to the east. Between 1903 and 1946, this land was used as a lairage for cattle passing through the market and is now used as a small industrial estate (see p. 124).

THE BROADWAY, Market Harborough, 1920s. In 1919 Market Harborough Urban District Council began its programme of building council houses by extending Clarence Street to the north and creating a small estate of ninety-eight houses on The Broadway, Hillside Road, Roman Camp Road and The Headlands.

GREAT BOWDEN ROAD, MARKET HARBOROUGH, 1930s. Between 1900 and 1930 private housing was developed rapidly along the main routes between the town and Great Bowden. This ribbon development was later consolidated by new private estates along Ridgeway Road, council estates on The Headlands and infill within the village itself. As a result Great Bowden is today physically integrated with Harborough, although its residents still maintain a strong sense of separate identity.

AERIAL VIEW OF GREAT BOWDEN, c. 1950. This village was the progenitor of Market Harborough and at the time of the Norman Conquest was the centre of a major royal estate in south Leicestershire. The plan of the village is very complex, with a number of greens surviving from the mediaeval period. Since this photograph was taken a considerable amount of development has taken place on the many cultivated spaces close to the roads.

CHURCH LANE, Dingley, 1920s. These are a good example of 19th-century estate cottages. They were built for staff at Dingley Hall by Viscount Downe. This road was formerly known as Hall Gardens.

ASHLEY ROAD, Albany, c. 1911. Looking north to the junction with Middle Lane.

THE DARBY ARCH, Wilbarston, c. 1900. This arch carries the road from Stoke Albany to Wilbarston. Through it runs one of the small picturesque watercourses which rise from the many local springs and flow north to feed the River Welland.

THE CROSSROADS, Wilbarston, c. 1910. Looking north from Main Street. There is a fine example of a village butcher's shop on the left, with an unglazed grill on the door to provide ventilation.

ROCKINGHAM CASTLE, 1906. Perched on the southern escarpment of the valley edge, the castle is a well-known local landmark visible from many of the villages. This spectacular and naturally defended site has been occupied since Roman times but the present castle is a royal construction and dates from the Norman Conquest. The gatehouse is one of several mediaeval extensions and dates from the 1280s.

ROCKINGHAM VILLAGE, c. 1910. Looking south down the steep main street, the north side of the Welland Valley can be seen in the distance. Rockingham is a good example of an estate village which has been owned by one family for generations, in this instance, the Watsons.

HIGH STREET, Great Easton, c. 1904. In contrast to Rockingham, Great Easton has never been dominated by a major resident landowner and this can be seen in the quantity of large houses built by wealthy yeomen farmers in the 17th and 18th centuries.

THE ROMAN WELL, Great Easton, c. 1910. This well is situated in a field to the north of the church, and is now filled in and dry. The superstructure was erected in the 18th century, incorporating part of the shaft from a churchyard cross.

THE BRIDGE, at Medbourne, c. 1920. This pack-horse bridge probably dates from the 13th century. Originally, it may have had parapet walls. In the foreground can be seen one of the many pipes which discharged raw sewage into the stream. This was a constant cause of diphtheria amongst local children until the late 1930s, when underground sewers were constructed. Piped water did not come to the village until the 1950s.

LOOKING EAST ACROSS THE GREEN, at Medbourne, c. 1920s. The bridge over the stream had just been rebuilt when this was taken and it was to be replaced by the present curved structure in the late 1950s. At about the same time the cottages on the extreme right were condemned and were left derelict until being cleared to extend the Green in the 1970s.

THE CROSS, Hallaton, c. 1900. The Butter Cross dates from the 17th century and is the last reminder of the weekly market held in the village until the 1800s. Behind the Butter Cross was the home of one of the two village doctors. The one resident here usually dealt with sick club patients, whom he treated in a surgery in a shed at the rear of the house.

HIGH STREET, Hallaton, c. 1910. The building with its gable end on the road was the former brewhouse of the Angel Hotel, a leading village inn during the 19th century. The three bays of the thatched building to the left formed the main body of the inn. The rest of the block was taken up by the village post office, printing office and cycle and radio shop of Frederick Hawke. The pump was one of the four which supplied the village until the 1960s.

THE RAILWAY STATION, Hallaton, 1900s. In 1879 Hallaton was connected to the rail network with the construction of what was to become the Great Northern and London & North Western Railway Joint Line. This made Hallaton a very busy station. It was possible to join the 10 a.m. London express at Hallaton so long as a ticket was purchased the previous day. When the Market Harborough boxer Reggie Meen unsuccessfully fought Primo Carnera in the early 1930s, the result was sent in morse code between the signal boxes along the London line and then shouted around the village by 'Sporty' Payne, a local boxing enthusiast. The station finally closed in 1953.

THE VILLAGE GREEN, Glooston, c. 1900. The village hall now stands where the house on the right is. On the extreme left of the picture can be seen the Blue Bell pub (see p. 109).

THE CARDIGAN ARMS, CRANOE c. 1908. From 1882 to 1946 the pub and the butcher's shop to the left were run by three generations of the Vendy family. A few years before this photograph was taken the shop was built at a cost of £24. Prior to this the meat was prepared in the pub kitchen. The Vendys supplied meat to most of the villages within a few miles of Cranoe.

MAIN STREET, SLAWSTON, 1900s. Looking north west to the junction with the road to Welham.

WELHAM, 1920s. This photograph is taken from The Front, a field which adjoins the Welland and contains an important sheep-washing pit which served Slawston, Cranoe and Weston. The hedge in the middle distance marks the course of an ornamental canal dug in the 1720s by the squire, Francis Edwards, who also rebuilt most of the village at this time.

MAIN STREET, ASHLEY, C. 1910. Looking east towards the Middleton Road.

WESTON O11.

MAIN STREET, WESTON BY WELLAND, 1900s. The school was built in 1871 and the land on the left of the road was used for the village's first council houses in the early 1920s.

EAST SIDE OF LEICESTER ROAD, MARKET HARBOROUGH, 1910s. Development along the Leicester Road began in the early 20th century, when the Freehold Land Society had developed a small estate in Victoria Avenue. A private development planned to link this with Burnmill Road did not materialize.

FAIRLAWN, Fairfield Road, Market Harborough, c. 1900. This house was built for Robert Symington in 1886 by William Knight. It is typical of the rather ostentatious mansions built by the town's 'new money' on the northern outskirts.

MAIN STREET, Tur Langton, 1920s, looking east.

THE WINDMILL, Kibworth Harcourt, 1950s. This post mill was probably built in 1711 by Daniel Hutchinson. It ceased production in the 19th century but was saved from dereliction in 1936 by the Society for the Protection of Ancient Buildings.

ALBERT STREET, Kibworth Harcourt, 1900s. The gardens of the 'Old House' on the left are now occupied by Beech Tree Close.

CHURCH ROAD, Kibworth Beauchamp, c. 1910. Although Kibworth Harcourt and Kibworth Beauchamp have formed one continuous settlement for several centuries the two communities still retain rather separate identities. St Wilfred's church here has served both villages since the 1500s, but even today the congregation sits on either the Harcourt (north) or Beauchamp (south) sides of the nave.

THE BANK, Kibworth Beauchamp, c. 1910. Dominating this customary meeting place is George Lynn's store, which was the leading retail concern from the 1880s until it was bought out by Burton's of Nottingham in the late 1940s.

HIGH STREET, Kibworth Beauchamp, c. 1906. Looking east towards the Bank, a number of buildings still show this area to be an early part of the village. The left-hand building is a farmhouse owned by the Cook family, who sold milk at this time. The outer wall of the cob cottage on the right survives to this day.

SMEETON ROAD, Kibworth Beauchamp, c. 1906. Formerly known as Victoria Street, this road is lined with houses built during the rapid rise in population in the village which followed the opening of several hosiery factories in the 1890s, such as Poynor's, on the side street to the right.

PITT GARDENS, Smeeton Westerby, c. 1908. Smeeton and Westerby were separate hamlets until the 1790s and both were within Kibworth parish until 1852. The allotment gardens probably take their name from a gravel pit formerly on this site.

PERCY PRESTON'S BOATHOUSE, Kibworth Beauchamp, 1920s. This boat-hire business was based on the Grand Union Canal near to bridge No. 74, to the south of Kibworth Top Lock.

THE DEBDALE WHARF INN, 1920s. This wharf was the southernmost point on the Union Canal between 1797 and 1809, when it was extended to Market Harborough. During this period it was a major transhipment point for goods heading further south by road.

FOXTON LOCKS AND THE INCLINE PLANE BARGE LIFT, c. 1910. The canal was extended further south with the construction of Foxton Locks between 1810 and 1814. However their narrowness eventually led to the construction of the incline plane barge lift to bypass the locks. This was opened in 1900 but was not a commercial success, ceased operation in 1910 and was dismantled in 1928.

HARRY FOSTER'S BOATHOUSE AND BRIDGE NO.12, 1910s. This was a very popular leisure spot for the people of Market Harborough from the late 19th century. From the 1920s an adjoining transport cafe known as Uncle Tom's Night Club proved equally popular, if not infamous. The hump-backed bridge carrying the A6 road was rebuilt in 1958.

NORTHAMPTON ROAD, Market Harborough, 1920s. This southern main road out of the town has a very interesting selection of houses, from detached villas to rustic terraces. Note the milkman delivering from a churn on the cart.

GRANVILLE STREET, MARKET HARBOROUGH, C. 1927. This formed the southern boundary of the Freehold Land Society's second estate, begun in 1879. Like many others built by the society, the street is named after a leading Liberal politician, in this instance, the second Earl Granville.

OATS ARE HARVESTED WHILE THE SOUTHERN ESTATE GROWS, Market Harborough, 1953. The Southern Estate was started in 1949 and it was a deliberate policy to keep agricultural land in production until it was required for building.

OPENING THE SOUTHERN ESTATE'S SHOPS, Market Harborough, 1957. This group of shops on the Western Avenue was a planned amenity for the estate (see p. 124). They are being officially opened by Mr O. de Rousset Hall, Chairman of the Urban District Council.

CLIPSTON & OXENDON SIGNAL BOX, 1950s. The L&NWR line from Market Harborough to Northampton was opened in 1859 and was used by passenger traffic until 1960. Here the signal box is manned by Sidney Messam who worked on this line for several years.

THE GEORGE INN, Great Oxendon, c. 1895. It seems that the original inn occupied only the middle of these three houses.

HIGH STREET, Kelmarsh, 1920s. This picturesque row of cottages was severely damaged by fire on 4 May 1943.

KELMARSH VILLAGE SCHOOL, 1900s. This was erected in 1870. Boys over 7 years old from the village had the right to attend Clipston Grammar School (see p. 96).

ARTHINGWORTH, from the Kelmarsh Road, c. 1910.

ARTHINGWORTH HALL, c. 1910. The hall was originally built in the 18th century, but was badly damaged by fire in 1900 and was rebuilt in this chaste classical style. It was, however, demolished in the 1950s.

BRAYBROOKE, 1910s, looking north from the junction of Green Lane with Griffin Road.

THE REAR OF THE OLD RECTORY, Little Bowden, c. 1865. This photograph is one of a number of this interesting building of 1627 by the Harborough photographer John Payne Jennings, who was active between 1861 and 1870.

ST NICHOLAS' CHURCH, Little Bowden, 1890s and 1920s. In 1900 the curious wooden turret was replaced by a stone bell-cote, designed by G.F. Bodley.

SECTION TWO

A Living from the Land

This section looks at the agriculture of the Welland Valley, and the crafts and trades which have been practised in its towns and villages.

The Welland Valley has always been primarily an agricultural area, and until the 1940s, one which had an international reputation for the high quality of its pasture. Throughout the 19th century, and up to World War Two, the fattening of beef cattle and sheep was the prime concern of local farmers. This 'dog and stick' agriculture required great skill and judgement as it depended upon buying in unfattened 'stores', moving the beasts from field to field to prevent over-grazing, and selling on the improved stock in the summer and autumn markets.

This way of life was permanently disrupted by the demand for arable crops during World War Two, and the increasing governmental control of production thereafter. The result today is a much more mixed agrarian economy, with some grazing continuing along the bottom of the river valley.

A large number of crafts and trades were reliant upon the grazier economy, as well as fox hunting which benefited from the high quality turf, the lack of fields with arable crops and high, stock-proof hedges. In addition more general crafts could be found in most villages before the middle of this century. These relied heavily on manual dexterity and a thorough knowledge of how to work locally produced raw materials.

THE CHAMPION BEAST at the Harborough Fat Stock Show, 1954. Mr W. Hart proudly displays his prize steer: the end result of careful grazing on the Welland Valley pastures at Weston by Welland. The annual December fatstock show marked the end of the grazing season in the area.

MARKET HARBOROUGH CATTLE MARKET, c. 1912. This purpose-built market was opened in 1903 and within the first two years almost 100,000 head of cattle and sheep were sold. The 'settling rooms' in the background housed the market offices and were designed by the town's leading architects, H.G. Coales and H.W. Johnson.

LOCAL GRAZIERS INSPECTING THE MILL FIELD, near Medbourne, 1940s. The most famous piece of rich, old pasture in the Welland Valley was the Mill Field, outside Medbourne at the apex of the roads to Slawston and Hallaton. This field even escaped ploughing up during World War Two as it was used for experiments on its grass. Here members of the county's War Agricultural Committee inspect the field and one of its 'products'.

DRESSED FOR WORK on the Hayward family's farm, Arthingworth, 1930s. Reg Hayward, 'Sonny' Walden, Jack Gotch and his father take a break while at work in the fields.

SHEEP WASHING, Lubenham, C. 1923. The Welland Valley was used to fatten large numbers of sheep as well as cattle. During April and May of each year all the sheep had to be washed before clipping. Here washing is underway in one of the many pits built along the Welland.

SHEARING SHEEP BY HAND, Naseby, C. 1909. Here two shearers are using traditional hand clippers.

MECHANICAL SHEEP SHEARING at Prince Rupert's Farm, Naseby, c. 1909. Here members of the Bromell and Westaway families demonstrate the serious and fun sides of sheep shearing, using hand-cranked mechanical clippers.

MOVING INTO PRINCE RUPERT'S FARM, Naseby, 1898. Considerable numbers of farmers moved into the Welland Valley from elsewhere in England between the 1870s and 1930s. Here members of the Westaway family (Goswick, Harry and Underwood) are in the process of moving into Prince Rupert's Farm from Stratton, in Cornwall. All the stock, horses and furnishings were transported by railway to North Kilworth station, and then moved by road to the farm.

MILKING TIME AT HALL FARM, Shangton, 1950s. Although the raising of fatstock dominated local agriculture until the 1950s, considerable milk production was carried out, often with Dairy Shorthorn cattle as seen here.

MISS GERTRUDE MARSH ON HER MILK ROUND, Husbands Bosworth, 1917. The Marsh family produced their own milk and sold it around the village using this ingenious 'dairy pram'. Note the different sized measures hanging from the bucket in her hand.

HARVESTING HAY near Market Harborough, C. 1905. Hay was the only major crop grown in the Welland Valley and a good cut was crucial to the successful over-wintering of store beasts and as a cash crop. Here a good harvest is being gathered from a field which is now part of Watson Avenue on the Southern Estate.

TURNING HAY, Naseby, c. 1906. Here the newly mown hay is being turned to dry it. This photograph was taken by J.G. Hasdell who used to visit the villages around Naseby every year to take portraits of local people.

STACKING HAY, Weston by Welland, 1940s. Here the Hart family are building a stack from hay gathered up from rows using a sweep pulled by the horse.

HEDGE LAYING, Weston by Welland, 1940s. Here Mr Church is making a quickset hedge on the Hart family's farm. A well-laid hedge was the most effective (and cheapest) way of keeping grazing beasts in their fields.

HEDGE LAYING ALONG THE GOADBY ROAD, Glooston, late 1940s. Here Charles Neal shows off his skill at laying hedges, which won him several prizes at the Leicestershire Agricultural Show.

HEDGER AT WORK near East Carlton church, 1860s. This workman is doing an excellent job of bringing neatness and strength to this slightly overgrown hedge on the East Carlton Hall estate. The photograph was taken by William John Jennings of Market Harborough. Jennings lived in The Chestnuts in Little Bowden between the 1850s and 1880s and worked as a permanent way inspector on the Midland Railway. He specialized in photographing churches and these often include fascinating details of everyday life.

LIFTING POTATOES, Weston by Welland, 1940s. Government control of food production during World War Two forced many Valley farmers to plough up their pasture for corn and root crops. Here two Italian prisoners of war, Gigi and Damian help the Hart family to lift potatoes on Weston Farm.

BUILDING A POTATO CLAMP, Weston by Welland, 1940s. Here the potatoes are being piled up ready for covering with straw and soil to be stored in a 'clamp'.

PICKING FLAX, Lubenham, 1940s. Flax was another crop grown in the Valley during the war. There was a major processing works for the crop at Billing, near Northampton.

A CROP OF FLAX ON THE ROAD, Weston by Welland, 1940s. The bundles of flax had to be lashed to the truck with ropes running the length of its chassis.

STOOKING CORN, Weston by Welland, 1940s. There were many problems with the first few seasons of corn on the old pastures, not least the inexperience of many local farmworkers with ploughing and harvesting machinery. Here Margaret Hart and Kath Falkner are stooking corn at Weston Farm.

ITALIAN POWs AND THEIR GUARDS, Medbourne, c. 1944. From 1942 prisoners of war were put to work on farms throughout the country. There were a number of camps and hostels for POWs in the area, but many lived with farming families. German POW labour only began in 1944.

TWO VIEWS OF LIFE IN THE LAND ARMY, c. 1946. The Women's Land Army was re-established just before the outbreak of war to provide much needed extra labour on farms throughout Britain. Despite considerable chauvinism, Land Girls soon proved they could work as well as male farmworkers. Above, a Christmas party is in progress at the W L A hostel in Lubenham, while, below, Land Girls work out how to extricate a bogged down tractor.

DRILLING GRASS SEED, Church Langton, late 1940s. After the war some farms gradually returned to grazing fatstock, but most diversified production in accordance with government subsidies. This led to an increase of machinery on the farms and much more work for agricultural contractors, such as Mr Reed, seen here on the seed drill.

WESTAWAY MOTORS TRADE STAND at a local agricultural show, 1952. This well-known Naseby firm shows off the latest agricultural machinery.

CLIPPING A PRIZE MULE, Market Harborough, 1900s. This mule was bred at the stables of Sir Humphrey de Trafford at Hill Crest House, and is being clipped by the groom, Daniel Swift.

PACKING VEGETABLES AT EADY'S MARKET GARDEN, Market Harborough, 1920s. This business was situated in Great Bowden Road. Their tomatoes were renowned locally for their sweetness. The greenhouses were later converted for growing mushrooms.

DOVECOTE, Sutton Bassett, c. 1900. Before the 19th century, dovecotes were a common feature of many villages as the birds provided a constant source of meat, feathers and manure.

AT THE REAR OF CHURCH & SON, HIGH STREET, Market Harborough, c. 1900. Church & Son set up as corn merchants in the town in the 1850s and soon became one of the leading businesses serving the agricultural community. Until the 1960s, the firm was based in both the High Street and a former malthouse on the corner of Nelson Street and Fairfield Road. Here the firm's delivery waggon poses for the camera in Hind Yard at the rear of the High Street shop.

EATON & CO., High Street, Market Harborough, 1900s. This gunsmith and ironmongery business began in the town in the 1800s and undertook considerable work in repairing agricultural machinery, as witnessed by hay machinery in front of the shop.

FOX THE SADDLERS AT CLIPSTON, c. 1910. Until the 1950s, the main form of motive power for farm work and local transport was the horse, so that most villages supported at least one saddle and harness maker. Here George Fox (left) and his son Harold stand outside their home and workshop on the Harborough Road, Clipston.

THE FORGE AT MIDDLETON, 1915. Blacksmiths were not only essential for maintaining local horse-drawn transport, but also for making and repairing agricultural tools and domestic hardwear. With the advent of motor transport many blacksmiths became mechanics. Here two Samuel Swinglers, father and son, stand proudly outside their forge, which was built in 1868. Next to them stand their wives, Florence and Lydia.

WILLIAM FALKNER making riding boots, Market Harborough, 1920s. The Falkner family were making, selling and repairing boots and shoes in Market Harborough from the 1830s until 1987. From the early 1900s to the 1950s they specialized in making bespoke riding boots for the hunting community. Here William Falkner II (1867–1934) sits in his workroom behind the shop at 55 High Street displaying one of his products. This workroom has been recreated at the Harborough Museum.

THE WHIPPER-IN AND THE EARTHSTOPPER, at Glooston, 1956. Fox hunting has been a popular sport in the area since the 18th century, and a number of the country's leading hunts are active in the Welland Valley, especially the Fernie and the Pytchley. From the 1880s to the 1920s Market Harborough was a very important centre for top class hunting and the sport contributed greatly to the local economy in many ways. Here Bruce Durno, the Whipper-In of the Fernie Hounds confers with Charles Neal who undertook many duties for the hunt, including earthstopping.

HUNTING TAXIDERMIST, Market Harborough, 1910s. Tom Turner was a postman by profession, but he gained a considerable local reputation for his hobby of taxidermy. This skill proved very useful in a hunting area such as the Welland Valley and many local houses were decorated with trophies prepared in his home in School Lane, Market Harborough.

GROOMS AT 'THE HIND', Market Harborough, 1910s. During the hunting season, many of the inns of Market Harborough and the surrounding villages provided stabling for large numbers of horses. Here a number of the grooms employed to look after the horses pose in the yard to the rear of The Hind, on the High Street.

CLIPSTON WINDMILL, 1900s. Until early this century there were many windmills in use in villages on the uplands at the edge of the Welland Valley. Most were wooden post mills like this one, which stood on the road from Clipston to Marston Trussell. It was owned by the village baker, John Buswell, who decided to demolish it shortly after this photograph was taken. Here four children of the Wartnaby family are climbing on one of the sail frames. They were renowned for starting up the mill on Sunday afternoons while Mr Buswell was having his Sunday afternoon sleep.

MEDBOURNE WINDMILL, C. 1900. This mill stood on the road from Medbourne to Slawston until it was demolished in 1902. It dated from the 18th century and was unusual for this area as it was built of brick. It was over 60 feet high and capped by a curious triangular top made of oak boards. To the right is the derelict mill house.

THE BUSWELL BAKERY, Clipston, 1952. The Buswell family were the village bakers from the 19th century until the early 1960s. In 1952 Ralph Buswell and his son Philip were photographed at work and the following four pictures show most of the main stages in the production of a traditionally baked loaf of bread. Here, flour is carried into the bakehouse. By this date, the family did not mill their own flour, but bought it from Northampton.

THE BUSWELL BAKERY, Clipston, 1952. Each sack of flour is emptied into a wooden bin in the bakehouse (above). The dough is then mixed up in glazed stoneware bowls (pancheons). Once proved, it is weighed out into portions to make individual loaves (below), which are placed in baking tins.

THE BUSWELL BAKERY, Clipston, 1952. The tins filled with dough are then put into a hot oven using a wooden peel, seen above in use by Ralph Buswell. Once baked, the fresh bread is sold door to door around the village and the surrounding area (below). It was not until the late 1950s that the horse and cart was replaced by a motor van.

A DELIVERY AT THE VILLAGE SHOP AND POST OFFICE, Lubenham, c. 1912. Until the proliferation of motor cars in the 1960s, virtually every village possessed a shop and post office. In Lubenham, the Miller family ran such a business in Main Street from the 1900s until the 1970s. Here an assistant, Maud Lambert, takes a short break while helping with a goods delivery.

PATSY GARTON IN MOWSLEY, 1920s. Patsy Garton was a well-known character in the villages to the north-west of Market Harborough. A small-holder renowned as a rabbit catcher and drinker, he could turn his hand to a host of jobs and typifies the multiple occupations carried on by many villagers at the time. Here he poses outside one of his favourite pubs on a carting job for Hubbard, the Mowsley and Laughton carrier.

A CARRIER AND HIS FAMILY, Ilston on the Hill, c. 1900. Up to the 1940s, when motor buses and goods vehicles became widespread, most local goods were delivered by horse-drawn carriers' vans. There was a vast network of carriers who made regular trips between the villages and the towns. Here J.H. Higgs poses for the photographer with his family outside the Fox and Goose Inn at Ilston on the Hill. He was based originally in Leicester, but later moved to High Street, Kibworth Beauchamp.

A COACHMAN, Marston Trussell, 1861. This fine portrait shows the costume of a coachman on a small country estate. It was taken by the Revd William Law, who was incumbent of Marston Trussell between 1842 and 1900 and was a pioneer local photographer of considerable technical and artistic skill.

THE HARBOROUGH BUS at Naseby, 1914. The Harborough Bus was run by the Market Harborough and District Motor Traction Company, founded by Edward Sharpe in 1913. As such it was the first serious attempt to provide a public passenger service for the area around the town. Although financial problems during World War One caused the company to go into liquidation, the bus service continued as a private venture until 1921. The bus was a Commer WP2 chain-driven vehicle and had the registration number LH8834.

DELIVERY AND REMOVAL VANS, Market Harborough, c. 1937. These beautifully painted delivery vans belonging to a well-known Harborough furnishing firm are typical of the vehicles which gradually ousted the village carriers' business from the 1930s onwards.

THE POST OFFICE AND GARAGE, Naseby, 1920s. Between 1911 and 1946, the post office in Naseby was owned and run by Endor Halford whose skill in other trades makes him a fascinating example of village entrepreneurship. He was a trained tailor and a self taught photographer who produced his own local postcards. Between 1906 and 1939 he was local correspondent for the *Northampton Mercury*. After World War One he ran a petrol station as well as a motor bus service for passengers, seen here on the extreme right.

THE NASEBY CHIMNEYSWEEP, c. 1920. Tom Ringrose was the last of a family of chimney sweeps who served Naseby and the surrounding villages and country houses. His cart and tools were stored at the top of Frog's Row.

CRAFTSMEN ALL, Husbands Bosworth, c. 1890. This photograph was probably taken at a social gathering of the village's friendly society. Each man holds a glass of beer in one hand and a tool of his trade in the other. The crafts represented are, left to right: blacksmith, builder, gardener, publican, groom (?), plumber and carpenter.

REBUILDING SLAWSTON WINDMILL, c. 1910. Slawston mill stood to the south-west of the village and was probably built in the 18th century. Here it is undergoing a thorough refurbishment by Elsam Brothers of Stamford not for milling but as a landmark for the local hunts. The mill was destroyed by lightning in 1929.

WOODWORKERS, Husbands Bosworth, c. 1890. Until the 1950s timber was an essential material for buildings, vehicles and artefacts, and most villages would have a resident carpenter who also worked as a wheelwright, undertaker and joiner. In this fine group photograph most of the workers at Wells' woodyard pose for the camera holding a tool of their trade. Two of them have white aprons rolled up around their waists.

RESTORING SUTTON BASSETT CHURCH, 1861. During the latter half of the 19th century most churches of the Welland Valley were restored, often resulting in a complete rebuilding. At Sutton Bassett, this 12th- and 13th-century chapel of ease of Weston was going to be extensively altered to the plans of Henry Goddard of Leicester. However, public opposition resulted in just a rebuilding of the north wall and re-roofing.

WOMEN BRICKWORKERS, 1890s. The clays which underlie the Welland Valley have provided good raw material for bricks since the early 18th century. This early photograph of brickworkers somewhere on the south side of the valley shows the costume worn by women in the brickyards.

LITTLE BOWDEN BRICKWORKS, c. 1910. The brickworks at Little Bowden were established in the late 18th century, although the kiln seen here dates from a century later. 'Bricky tip' occupied the field to the east of Bellfield Street and finally ceased working in the 1920s. Besides building bricks, the works also produced land drains, which can be seen piled behind the group of workers.

QUARRYING AT NEVILLE HOLT LIMEPIT, C. 1952. During World War Two limestone was quarried from the ridge to the west of Neville Holt for agricultural use. Here Ted Barker is about to blast the quarry face.

SECTION THREE

Life in the Community

This section looks at many aspects of everyday life in the Welland Valley communities within the framework of our life cycle.

From birth to death our lives are linked with others in the local community in very many ways. The last hundred years have seen the origins and development of effective local government which has provided and enforced high standards of sanitation, power, housing and education for all. At the same time, however, greater personal mobility brought about by faster and cheaper transport has diluted the communal spirit in many villages.

The photographs begin with childhood, education, leisure and adulthood. The emphasis then shifts to communal action in religion, public service and the work of local government. Politics, war and its commemoration finally lead to old age and death.

CHILDREN IN THE STREETS, Main Street, Wilbarston, 1910s. The street culture of children has always been an important element of playing and learning, and until the present generation, children spent much of their free time out of doors in groups.

TRAFFIC-FREE STREETS, Main Street, Middleton, c. 1906. The decline of children's street culture has much to do with the development and proliferation of fast motor transport.

CHILD WITH A HOOP, Market Harborough area, c. 1883. The steel hoop was one of the many toys which needed to be played with in the street.

CHILD WITH A WHEELED TOY, Market Harborough area, c. 1883. Another wheeled toy, which also encouraged walking in small children. This and the photograph above were taken by G.A. Nichols, a Stamford based photographer who was active in the area in the 1880s.

STAFF AND PUPILS at Clipston Grammar School, c. 1875. Clipston Grammar School was founded in 1667 by Sir George Buswell. Boys from Clipston and the neighbouring villages of Kelmarsh, Great Oxendon, Marston Trussell, Haselbech and East Farndon were to be taught free in the school. Here the Headmaster, the Revd Boyd, stands in front of the main door with staff and pupils. Boys under the age of 7 and girls were educated at the village National School, established in 1862.

CLIPSTON GRAMMAR SCHOOL AND HOSPITAL, 1928. The combined school and almshouse was erected between 1668 and 1673 to designs of Matthew Cole of Clipston. Between 1926 and 1928 the interior was reorganized and separate almshouses built.

KIBWORTH GRAMMAR SCHOOL, Kibworth Beauchamp, 1910s. Reputed to have been established in the 15th century, the school has definitely been functioning since 1559, although it did not occupy a special building until about 1630. A new schoolroom and master's house, seen here, was built in 1725. The third storey was added in the 1830s.

CHILDREN OUTSIDE DINGLEY SCHOOL, 1880s. The small school building, typical of those in many villages, was built in 1842. The teacher seen here is Mary Ann Elliott. Another photograph by G.A. Nichols.

ARTHINGWORTH SCHOOL, 1900s. This school, on the right of the picture, was established in 1733 as a result of a charitable bequest of William Marriott.

SEWING APPRENTICES taught by the Misses Crane, Market Harborough, 1888. Annie and Mary Ann Crane were two sisters who worked as dressmakers from their house on the Coventry Road. They also taught sewing and dressmaking to young women. Here a group of pupils/apprentices show off some of their products.

CHILDREN'S GARDENING COMPETITION at Weston by Welland, 1950s. Many local agricultural shows and societies included competitions designed to teach children agricultural skills. Here children are either hoeing turnips or singling beet at a competition organized by the Hallaton Agricultural Society.

ATHLETICS CLASS FOR CORSETRY WORKERS, Market Harborough, 1916. The corsetry firm of R. & W.H. Symington was renowned for providing sports and educational facilities for its workforce, many of whom started work at the age of 12 or 13. Here Perrygold Symington, a sister of R. and W.H. Symington, presides over an athletics class of junior workers.

LUBENHAM BOY SCOUTS DRUM & FIFE BAND, at Sulby Hall, 17 August 1913. The Scout Movement began in the 1900s with the deliberate intention of teaching moral and practical skills to children. Here the Lubenham scout band poses for a photograph after parade at Sibbertoft church. They had been inspected by Guy Paget and then given dinner at camp in the grounds of his home: jam pudding, roast beef and potatoes.

A DANCING CLASS AT FOXTON, 1949. Dancing has always been a popular way of socializing in both town and village. Here a class for the youth of Foxton is in progress, taught by Miss P. Stretton (left in the near right-hand couple) and organized by Miss L. Clarke (right).

ASSEMBLY ROOMS, Abbey Street, Market Harborough, 1950s. The Assembly Rooms were the main venue for organized dances, hunt balls and many other social events for the area. They were built in 1903, replacing the corn exchange of 1858. In the 1960s they were demolished to be replaced by the Edinburgh House offices.

PRESENTING PRIZES AT A ROCK 'N ROLL DANCE, Market Harborough, 1957. The 1950s saw the birth of the 'teenager' and a distinct 'pop' music in rock 'n roll. Here O. de Rousset Hall, Chairman of the Urban District Council, looks slightly out of place presenting prizes at a rock 'n roll dance.

FUN FAIR ON THE FORMER BREWERY LAND, Northampton Road, March 1939. From the middle of the 19th century until the 1960s fun fairs visited the town regularly each April and October. Until the mid-1930s, they were sited on the Square.

FIRST SATURDAY MATINEE FOR THE ABC MINORS, Ritz Cinema, Northampton Road, Market Harborough, c. 1950. From the 1920s to the 1960s the cinema was one of the main places of entertainment in the town. The first cinema, the County Electric, opened in 1911 and stood on the Square, where Woolworths now stands. Ten years later the Oriental (later the Orien) opened in St Mary's Road, and was the town's leading cinema until Associated British Cinemas built the Ritz in 1939. The County closed within a few months, but the town continued to patronize two cinemas until 1959, when the Orien closed. The Ritz itself closed in 1978. ABC formalized Saturday matinees for juniors by starting the ABC Minors Club, with older children as monitors to try and keep order. These are distinguished here by their armbands.

TEATIME BY THE CANAL, Foxton (above) and the Harborough Arm (below), 1910s. The nearby stretch of the Grand Union Canal was very popular for individual or group excursions on foot or by boat – not to mention courting couples! Many of the houses adjoining the canal cashed in on this by opening tea rooms and hiring out boats. Also local photographers set up booths to provide a record of an outing or a loved one.

A FASHIONABLE WEDDING, Market Harborough, c. 1907. Here Lizzie Gardiner (centre) celebrates her wedding with Alf Hodby (back left). Her three sisters act as bridesmaids. Their father, George Gardiner, was a well-known town shopkeeper (see p. 12).

MEMBERS OF THE CONGREGATIONAL CHAPEL SUNDAY SCHOOL set out on an excursion, St Mary's Road, Market Harborough, 1900s. The Congregational ('Top') Chapel ran an extensive Sunday school programme for both children and adults. Every other year it organized a major excursion, requiring a hired railway train. Here leading members march to the station led by the chapel band and followed by the Sunday school banner.

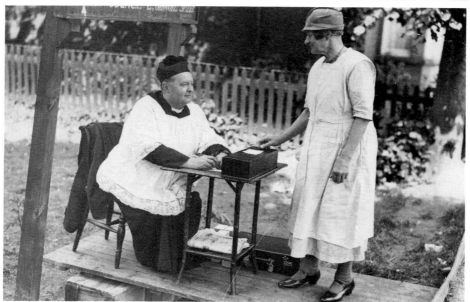

GIFT DAY FOR ST HUGH'S CHURCH, Northampton Road, Market Harborough, June 1937. The rapid development of the town along the Northampton Road from the 1880s overstretched the resources of Little Bowden parish, and in 1892 a mission room was opened in Granville Street. In 1895 a temporary corrugated iron church was also erected and then a long campaign to raise money for a permanent church began. This was finally accomplished by 1938 and the building was consecrated in 1940. Here Revd G.A.A. Finch receives a donation from a parishioner.

THE LEICESTER DIOCESE CHURCH ARMY VAN in the Welland Valley, 1920s. This van toured the county and provided a base for members preaching in the country districts.

THE OFFICIAL OPENING OF THE BAPTIST CHAPEL, Coventry Road, Market Harborough, 25 March 1907. The Baptists had worshipped here since 1830, but in 1907 this larger and better furnished chapel was built, extending the earlier one, which was some way back from the road. The chapel was designed by George Baines.

A TABLEAU FROM A MISSIONARY PAGEANT, Langton Villa, Great Bowden, 1920s. In the late 1920s and early 1930s, many local churches combined to perform pageants about, and in aid of, overseas missionary work. Here people from Great Bowden re-enact their tableau from a pageant originally held in the Assembly Rooms at Market Harborough.

THE CHEQUERS INN, Tur Langton, c. 1906. For centuries the local pub has been a major focus for local social life and every village in the Valley had at least one pub. Much business was done under their roofs and the local friendly societies used pubs as semi-official offices.

THE WEST SIDE OF THE GREEN at Medbourne, c. 1920. The Neville Arms is in the background, and the sapling planted on the green commemorates the coronation of George V in 1911. A village green overlooked by a pub may seem a romantic cliché of 'olde Englande', but in most Welland Valley villages the two seem to go together. Probably the result of hard headed commerce as most outdoor village events would take place on the green, so providing many thirsty clients.

THE BLUE BELL PUBLIC HOUSE, at Glooston, c. 1900. At this time the pub was run by George and Mary Neal. The postman on the left was based in Market Harborough and served a group of villages from the Langtons to Slawston.

POSTMAN TOM TURNER, 1920s. Tom Turner worked most of his life for the Post Office delivering mail to villages north-east of Market Harborough. Here he proudly displays his long service medal. In his spare time he practised taxidermy (see p. 78).

THE KIBWORTH HARCOURT POST OFFICE, 1910s. Besides the local pub, the post office has been the other key community facility in Welland Valley villages. Here C.W. Cooper (far right) the sub postmaster of Kibworth Harcourt poses for the camera with his staff. Cooper worked with a local photographer to produce his own postcards.

STOKE ALBANY POST OFFICE, 1900s. This small post office was run by George Watts.

AN ARMISTICE PARADE, KIBWORTH BEAUCHAMP, 1920s. The parade is led by Superintendent Mee and Sergeant Larkins of the Harborough Division of the Leicestershire Constabulary.

HARBOROUGH FIREMEN AND BOY SCOUTS MARCH TO THE CORONATION CELEBRATIONS along the High Street, Market Harborough, 1911.

CLEARING UP AFTER THE TANNERY FIRE, the Commons, Market Harborough, 1905. The tannery, which occupied the Commons area of the town from the early 19th century to 1914, was prone to frequent fires. This one was particularly extensive.

HARBOROUGH FIRE BRIGADE DEMONSTRATING ITS NEW STEAM FIRE ENGINE, Church Square, Market Harborough, 1905. The firemen are about to test the power of the water jet against the height of the church tower.

HARBOROUGH FIRE BRIGADE SHOWS OFF ITS EQUIPMENT, C. 1905 The first official volunteer fire brigade in the town was raised in 1870. From 1880 until 1948 it was under the control of the local council, and then became part of the Leicestershire Fire Service. All the equipment seen here was paid for by public subscription.

HARBOROUGH FIRE BRIGADE WITH TROPHIES, 1920s. The local brigade was a frequent winner in regional and national competitions. The firemen here are, back row, left to right: Harry Haddon, Cecil Sturgess, George Allmark, Dick Kelly. Front: Albert Payne, Fred Allen, Harry Payne and Mr Rayworth.

INSPECTOR THOMAS GRAIN riding an early scooter, c. 1920. Thomas Grain joined the Leicestershire Constabulary in 1887 and was in charge of the Market Harborough police station from 1914 to 1921.

MARKET HARBOROUGH POLICE HOUSE, King's Road, c. 1914

HALLATON'S VILLAGE POLICEMAN, 1950s. PC George (Jack) Seaman served as the village 'bobby' from 1942 to 1956. In addition to Hallaton, his beat included seventeen surrounding villages, for which his bicycle was the only form of transport.

MARKET HARBOROUGH'S FIRST WOMAN POLICE CONSTABLE, c. 1950. WPC Lamley helps children from Fairfield Road School cross the High Street.

STEAM DISINFECTING UNIT, St Luke's Hospital, Market Harborough, 1934. The casual ward at St Luke's hospital attracted many 'gentlemen of the road' on the tramp along the A6. This unit was built to disinfect their clothes while staying at the hospital.

FILLING IN THE LITTLE BOWDEN BRICKWORKS PIT, 1938. With the closure of the brickworks in the 1920s these clay workings to the east of Glebe Road became a deep (and dangerous) pond. It was finally filled in by the District Council using household refuse.

MARKET HARBOROUGH GAS WORKS, Clarence Street, 1957. The gas works were built in 1833 by a private company, which was bought out by the Urban District Council in 1899. After a number of expansions the works were made part of the East Midlands Gas Board system in 1949. They closed down after the town was 'converted' to natural gas in December 1969.

HIGH STREET, HALLATON C. 1920. The fine Georgian house at the top of the street was sited on a spring which partly fed the conduit near the Cross. This and a number of pumps provided the village's water supply until the 1960s.

WATER BORE HOLE PUMP, Husbands Bosworth, 1936. Until 1890, Market Harborough's water came from private pumps and wells which were often very polluted. Then the local council created a piped supply drawn from bore holes near Husbands Bosworth. This supply system was gradually increased until 1962 when the town was joined to Leicester's supply. Here J.G. Barlow, the council's surveyor stands next to the pump of No. 10 well which had just been installed.

OLD AND NEW COURSES OF THE JORDAN BROOK, Braybrooke Road Bridge, Little Bowden, May and July 1957. Flooding along the river Welland and its main local tributary, the Jordan brook, was a regular problem until the 1960s, when a comprehensive prevention scheme was carried out. The realignment carried out here was an early part of the scheme which, however, did not prevent a major flood on 2 July 1958.

MARKET HARBOROUGH SWIMMING BATHS, Northampton Road, 1896. These public baths were created through the generosity of the local MP, J. W. Logan, who offered to contribute £1,000 towards their cost if a public appeal could raise a similar sum. This was achieved quickly and the Urban District Council built and staffed the baths. Until the 1950s the building provided washing and laundry facilities as well as a swimming pool. The baths were closed when the Harborough Leisure Centre opened in August 1991.

'ALMHOLME', Abbey Street, Market Harborough, 1957. This interestingly shaped house was built in the 1870s to conform to the boundaries of one of the long thin 'burgage plots', laid out in the mediaeval period, fronting High Street. Abbey Street was a new road created in 1901 as a link road from New Harborough to the middle of the High Street.

THE OPENING CEREMONY FOR ROMAN WAY, 1936. Roman Way was built as a link road between Church Square and the council estate on The Broadway. Here the street sign is about to be unveiled by Cllr H.H. Pickering.

THE FIRST OFFICIAL PEDESTRIANS ON ROMAN WAY, Market Harborough, 1936. Here Cllr E.W. Thompson, H.G. Coales (the surveyor) and Cllr H. H. Pickering lead the walkers. Roman Way takes its name from a nearby Anglo-Saxon enclosure which was incorrectly thought to be Roman by early antiquaries.

THE ANCIENT FOOTPATH ACROSS BOWDEN FIELDS, Market Harborough, August 1945. This trackway links Great Bowden and Lubenham via Market Harborough, where it runs down Kings Road, crosses the High Street, goes through the yard of the Three Swans and then heads west over the site of New Harborough. Its course across Bowden Fields is now partially obscured by the estate built between 1945 and 1949.

OFFICIAL OPENING OF THE FIRST HOUSES ON THE BOWDEN FIELDS ESTATE, Market Harborough, 28 November 1946. This estate provided one hundred much-needed homes at the end of the war. Although the first house was occupied in 1946, shortage of building materials held up the work and the estate was not completed until 1949. Here members of the Urban District Council welcome the first tenant with a set of saucepans.

PREFABS ON THE LAIRAGE, Market Harborough, February 1946. Another way the council attacked the town's post-war shortage of housing was to erect twenty-seven 'Spooner' prefabs on the cattle lairage by Dingley Terrace. These houses remained in use until 1968 when they were replaced by a small industrial estate.

THE OFFICIAL OPENING OF THE SOUTHERN ESTATE, Market Harborough, 1 February 1951. All the roads on this estate are named after leading figures in the Civil War. It was appropriate therefore that it was formally opened by Mrs H.B. Lenthall, a lineal descendant of the Speaker of Parliament in 1645, William Lenthall. The architect of the estate was Lyndon Rowen.

THE FIRST TENANT OF THE SOUTHERN ESTATE, Market Harborough, August 1953. Mrs Stocks moved into her new home in 7 Stuart Road in February 1951. The Urban District Council had planned an estate of about 700 homes to the south of the town in the early 1940s, but work did not commence until 1949. By 1953 180 houses had been built and by 1956 a further 150 dwellings had been erected by private developers. The following year a shopping centre on the Western Avenue was completed (see p. 51).

A VILLAGE DISTRICT NURSE OUTSIDE HER HOME, Gumley, c. 1930. Between the wars, Ethel Carter worked as a district nurse and midwife for the villages of Lubenham, Gumley, Theddingworth, Laughton and Mowsley. She retired in the late 1940s, after many years of service.

THE OFFICIAL OPENING OF THE ST JOHN AMBULANCE STATION, Abbey Street, Market Harborough, 1924. Until the 1940s the St John Ambulance Brigade was the only body providing local transport for the sick. From 1913 until this station was built, the Brigade stored its equipment in the Fire Station across the road.

THE FIRST AND SECOND PHASES OF THE COTTAGE HOSPITAL, Coventry Road, Market Harborough, c. 1913 (top) and c. 1920. Free nursing for the poor began in the town in 1885 when a charity was established to employ a district nurse. In 1909 the printer George Green gave land for the present cottage hospital, which was built by 1910. In 1920 an appeal was launched for the first of many extensions to the building. This was to act as a war memorial and the wing was opened in 1924. Both phases were designed by H.G. Coales.

MARKET HARBORO' WAR MEMORIAL~COTTAGE HOSPITAL EXTENSION
Shewing proposed additions to the Right of "X".

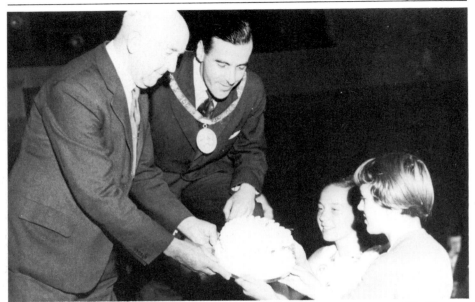

'ABC MINORS' PRESENT A BIRTHDAY CAKE AND PRESENT TO THE COTTAGE HOSPITAL, Ritz Cinema, Market Harborough, 1957. This is one of many events which were held every year until the 1970s to raise funds for the cottage hospital.

COLLECTING MONEY FOR THE COTTAGE HOSPITAL ON CARNIVAL DAY, 1933. The Harborough Carnival was the most important fund-raising event of the hospital's benefit. Here members of the Harborough Young Men's Friendly Society have donned fancy dress and are collecting in the streets with a barrel organ. They are (l–r), -?-, Borris Fitzjohn, Dick Branston, Bert Haddon.

DORIS GILBERT: THE FIRST CARNIVAL QUEEN, 1931. Although there had been a number of special charity carnivals for the hospital during the 1920s, the 1931 carnival was the first to be organized on present day lines with a parade of floats and the selection of a Carnival Queen. This portrait (right), taken by T.A. Kay in his studio in Northampton Road, was sent to the judges and won Doris the title. She was crowned, on a float supplied by Tomlinson the coal merchant, by Lady Lock-Elliott of Hallaton (below). Her costume was made by the staff at R. & W.H. Symington, where she worked in the brassière department.

THE WINNING FLOAT AT THE 1933 HARBOROUGH CARNIVAL. This float was entered by R. & W. H. Symington and depicts 'Lady Liberty' – a pun on the Liberty Bodices made at the factory and worn by the children on the float. The part of the Lady was played by Miss V. Roberts from the White Room. This float had to be redirected during the parade as it was too tall to pass under the Northampton Road railway bridge.

THE MARKET HARBOROUGH TOC H FLOAT at the 1938 Carnival. Mr F.J. Phillips is in drag as an alternative Carnival Queen.

A TOC H FESTIVAL at the Assembly Rooms, Market Harborough, 7 June 1947. The Christian organization Toc H was very popular in the area during the period between the wars. A group was founded in Market Harborough in December 1926 and within two years it had established a meeting room in a disused bottling store at the rear of the Angel Hotel. Meetings were held here every Tuesday and the group planned many activities to help or raise money for the unemployed, offenders and local charities. By 1938 the branch had over fifty members and a Welland District was established for the four other branches in villages along the Valley. This photograph was taken during the Branch's 21st birthday celebrations. It shows Harry Edwards speaking to an invited audience at the Assembly Rooms. The group is still active today, although it has far fewer members.

A PRESENTATION OF THE MARKET HARBOROUGH CITIZENSHIP CUP to the Market Harborough Archaeological and Historical Society, 17 October 1957. The Citizenship Cup was given to the Urban District Council anonymously in 1955 to mark its diamond jubilee. It was to be awarded from time to time to individuals or organized groups in recognition of outstanding achievement, enhancing the reputation of Market Harborough and for distinguished service rendered in the interest of the town. To date, the cup has been awarded six times: to H.H. Pickering, a long-time chairman of the council and many other committees; the Market Harborough Archaeological and Historical Society; Ernest Elliott, the local entertainer; George Aldridge, the local boxer who won the British Middleweight Championship; the Market Harborough Division of the St John Ambulance Brigade; and Reginald Crisp, for work with the elderly. With the reorganization of local government in 1974, the award ceased, although currently there are plans for it to be re-established.

JOHN MARCH, CHURCHWARDEN FOR TWENTY-EIGHT YEARS, Great Bowden, 8 June 1980. Here John March receives a token of appreciation from the vicar, Revd Boyce, and leading parishioners of Great Bowden for his long service as churchwarden.

MARKET HARBOROUGH LABOUR LEAGUE OF YOUTH, 1951. Here members meet with Mr T.C. Boyd, the prospective Labour candidate for the Harborough Constituency at the general election. Boyd gained 21,648 votes, but came second to the Conservative candidate, Mr J.M. Baldock, who got 29,395 votes.

LOCAL MEMBERS OF THE NORTHAMPTONSHIRE YEOMANRY, probably at Slough, 1914. Four members of local farming families prepare to 'do their bit' for king and country. They are, left to right: Billy West of East Farndon, Tom Tibbits of Clipston, Robert Swinfen of Kelmarsh and Frank Jones.

SIBBERTOFT WOMEN SEWING SOLDIERS' COMFORTS, during World War One.

MEXICANS AT THE MARKET HARBOROUGH REMOUNT DEPOT, August 1917. During the war the Cattle Market was converted to a Remount Depot for army horses. Three Mexican soldiers came to work here in 1917 and soon became popular heroes and heart-throbs for their daring riding and lasso stunts performed at local charity events. Above, Pablos Ramos demonstrates his skill with a rope, while below he prepares to give a riding demonstration with Claudio Coborrubius and Carlos Mier.

INVALID SOLDIERS at West Langton Hall, c. 1916. During World War One Mr H.G. Mills made West Langton Hall available to the military for use as a convalescent home. Here recuperating soldiers in their distinctive dark blue uniforms pose in front of the hall with local children.

AMERICAN SERVICEMEN, somewhere in Market Harborough, June 1944. Here members of the B Battery 456 Parachute Field Artillery, of the United States' Army's 82nd Airborne Division pose for a photograph before leaving for the D-Day landings in Normandy.

HMS *FERNIE,* entering Bergen harbour, 25 May 1946. Fernie was a Hunt Class destroyer built in Glasgow in 1940 and 'adopted' by the Market Harborough area in 1942. During a month of fund-raising in February and March of that year £150,000 was raised on her behalf. *Fernie* was the second of 86 Hunt Class destroyers to be built, all named after British packs of foxhounds – a clever way of enlisting local support for the boats. *Fernie* served the whole of the war in North Atlantic waters and undertook a wide variety of tasks including the evacuation of Cherbourg and Le Havre after the Fall of France, the raids on Bruneval and Dieppe, the D-Day landings and providing convoy escort. At the end of the war she was disarmed and used as a target vessel with the Fleet Air Arm. *Fernie* was finally scrapped in 1956.

EVACUEE CHILDREN RECEIVING MILK, Market Harborough, September 1939. Here Elsie Gardiner hands bottles of milk to some of the 3,250 children who were evacuated to the Harborough area from London at the beginning of World War Two.

PARENTS OF EVACUEE CHILDREN visit Husbands Bosworth, c. 1940, and meet the villagers who were looking after them.

DEDICATION OF A WAR MEMORIAL SEAT on the Green, Great Bowden, late 1940s.

RE-DEDICATING THE LUBENHAM WAR MEMORIAL, 1949. This memorial was originally built opposite Westgate Lane, but was moved to the site of the village pond (see p. 15) when it was re-dedicated for those killed in World War Two.

THE SMEETON INSTITUTE, Theddingworth, 1900s. This building, which now acts as the village hall, was built in 1893 by John Smeeton as a village reading and recreation room in memory of his son Sydney Perry Smeeton who died in 1889.

ALMSPEOPLE, Clipston, c. 1870. The Headmaster of Clipston Grammar School and Hospital poses with his wife and some of the 'twelve poor persons' for whom the almshouses were built (see p. 96). A photograph by W. Daynes of Rugby.

MRS EXTON, Hallaton, 1890s. In the 18th century two charities were established to provide almscottages for poor widows. Mrs Exton was living in one of these cottages when she was photographed. She was renowned for her strict religious views, collecting for foreign missions and regular attendance at church.

MR & MRS ROBIN LOUNT, Hallaton, 1890s. This elderly couple were photographed at the same time as Mrs Exton. Their aged status in the community is perhaps emphasized here by the pattens placed on the ground beside them. These were considered very old fashioned footwear by this time.

HORSE-DRAWN HEARSE, at a funeral in the Harborough area, 1920s.

THE FUNERAL OF CORPORAL M. G. BERRY, Great Bowden, November 1940. Cpl Berry was only nineteen when he died of meningitis while at camp and was brought home to Great Bowden for burial.

Ceremony and Celebration

This section looks first at group sports and pastimes, and then deals with some of the regular events in the communal calendar of the Welland Valley. It concludes with national celebrations in war and peacetime.

Photographers in the past seem to have concentrated excessively on recording public events in the villages and countryside of the Valley. But this is not to deny the importance of calendar customs, sports and public celebrations in fostering and maintaining a sense of communal identity.

This certainly seems to have been in the minds of many squires, parsons and teachers of the 19th century who promoted sports clubs and 'revived' traditional customs in their villages. Ironically, the Hallaton Bottle Kicking ceremony, which is the most famous calendar custom in the area, was frequently attacked by the same community leaders – perhaps because its truly traditional rowdiness did not conform with their 'hidden agenda' of social control.

THE GREAT EASTON CORONATION BRASS BAND, C. 1902. No procession is complete without a band in the lead. This band was established for Edward VII's coronation by the corset manufacturer, William Fox Haddon (centre). It was disbanded in 1939.

THE WESTON BY WELLAND CRICKET TEAM, late 1890s. Village clergy were often instrumental in setting up village cricket teams during the 19th century, to enhance community spirit and teach a sense of 'fair play'.

LUBENHAM ALBION FOOTBALL TEAM at Great Glen, c. 1926. Village football teams were another great source of local pride and rivalry.

THE VICAR OF NASEBY TRYING TO 'KILL THE RAT' at the village fête, 1950s. The annual fête provides an opportunity to have fun, raise money and develop the organizational skills of the villagers. Here the Revd Mansell tries to win a prize by hitting a 'rat' of wood dropped through the drainpipe.

FOX HOUNDS AT WILBARSTON, 1910s. The Welland Valley has been an important area for fox hunting since the 18th century. Here members of the Woodland Pytchley Hunt set off down Scott Lane in pursuit of 'the inedible'.

A POLO ENTHUSIAST AND HIS GROOM, Arthingworth, 1930s. Norman Perkins (right) lived at Arthingworth Hall between the wars and did much to promote polo in the area. Here Mr J. Masters holds his mount while he takes a break during a match at the polo field opposite the junction of the Clipston and the Northampton roads.

JUDGING HUNTERS AT CLIPSTON SHOW, c. 1930. The annual Clipston and District Flower Show began in 1910 and in 1926 an agricultural section was added, under the patronage of the Duke of York (later George VI). The show declined in the late '30s and ceased in 1938.

JUDGING POTATOES at the Hallaton Agricultural Society root show, 1950s. This society was established in 1947 for those interested in improving farming methods. Besides lectures it originally held annual shows for root crops as well as organizing sheep shearing and hedge laying competitions.

SINGING AROUND WILLIAM HUBBARD'S TOMB, St Mary in Arden, 1919. In 1786 William Hubbard, a market gardener, left the choir of Market Harborough parish church a guinea a year on condition it sang a hymn around his grave each Easter eve. The ceremony is still carried out.

HALLATON BOTTLE KICKING: THE PARADES, 1900s. Until the 1950s, the three main friendly societies in the village (Oddfellows, Hallaton Friendly Society and the Tuxford Club) would parade through the village on the morning of the bottle kicking ceremony. The village band was joined by the Wigston band and the money collected went to society funds. Here society members are returning from the morning service at the church to have lunch in the pubs where they held meetings (the Royal Oak, the Fox and the Bewick Arms respectively).

HALLATON BOTTLE KICKING: DRESSING THE BOTTLES, 1930s. The Hallaton Bottle Kicking and Hare Pie Scramble is a long established custom which takes place every Easter Monday. Here three 'bottles' (small wooden casks filled with beer) have just been decked with ribbon provided by the village drapers shop. On the extreme left stands Laurence Kitchen with a sack ready to receive the hare pie. Holding the bottles are, left to right: 'Butcher' Marlow, Walter Brown and George Neal (the Bottle Keeper). Beside him stands Mrs Neal, his aunt.

HALLATON BOTTLE KICKING: THE PARADE, 1920s. After being dressed, bottles and a large hare pie are paraded through the village via the Fox pub at the top green. Here the parade is returning from the Fox along High Street towards the rectory for blessing. The bottles are held aloft in the middle of the crowd.

HALLATON BOTTLE KICKING: BLESSING THE PIE, C. 1905. The hare pie is blessed and cut up by the Rector before the main ceremony and contest on Hare Pie Bank. Today this is done on the churchyard steps, but formerly took place at the rectory. Here the Revd James Preece officiates surrounded by members of the Neal family who were bearers and keepers of the bottles for several generations.

HALLATON BOTTLE KICKING: THE CONTEST, 1953. The main action of the day takes place on Hare Pie Bank, a steep field rising from a stream on the south of the village. Here the diced hare pie is thrown to the crowd and each of the bottles is fought for by two teams: one from Hallaton, and the other from neighbouring Medbourne (with anyone else who wishes to join in). Here Eric Clipston is running from a scrummage with one of the bottles.

HALLATON BOTTLE KICKING: WINNING A POINT, c. 1910. The aim of the contest is to carry the bottle either across the stream below the Bank (a Hallaton win) or over the field towards Medbourne. Here combatants are standing by the stream at the bottom of Hare Pie Bank after a winning point. They are watched over by the village policeman, PC Mayes. Between the 1880s and the 1930s Hallaton won every contest, but then started to lose when Medbourne recruited Scottish steelworkers from nearby Corby.

HALLATON BOTTLE KICKING: THE WINNING SIDE, c. 1900. The side which scores with two out of the three bottles is the winner of the day. This often takes the whole afternoon and early evening. The combatants then process back to the Butter Cross, where a leading member of the winning side is seated on the top and the contents of the bottle are drunk.

MISS ETHEL FOX WITH A MAY DAY GARLAND, Clipston, 1950s. Many village May Day customs were revived in the 19th century by heritage-conscious clergy and teachers. Here Miss Fox stands next to the 'traditional' May garland carried around Clipston by four young children while soliciting money. Its design and the accompanying song were drawn up in the 1860s by her mother, the village schoolmistress.

THE BRAYBROOKE GARLAND, 1919. Another version of a May Day Garland.

MAY QUEEN PROCESSION, Naseby, 1931. The May Queen is Mary Toseland and leading the horse is Francis 'Chicken' Adnett (because he had a long nose!), the local carpenter and wheelwright. It is interesting that most of the people in this procession are from families of farm workers or tradespeople, rather than farm owners.

WHITSUNTIDE PROCESSION, Sibbertoft, 1900s. Every Whitsuntide members of the village women's clothing club would be paid in material and garments and process around the village, led by the vicar and the band. In the evening there would be a dance in the club room of the Red Lion pub. Members of many families living away would come home for this holiday.

ANCIENT ORDER OF FORESTERS at Medbourne, 1900s. Before the coming of the Welfare State, friendly societies played a major role in the lives of most working people. Their pseudo rituals and regalia added considerable colour to many village highdays and holidays. Here the Medbourne Foresters have emerged from the Neville Arms ready for a procession, probably during the Whitsun holiday.

CONTESTANTS AT A PLOUGHING MATCH, Sibbertoft, 1890s. Ploughing matches were commonly held around the Valley in spring.

THE ANNUAL MOWING OF THE CHURCHYARD at Braybrooke, 1950s.

THE ANNUAL TENANTS' LUNCHEON, Deene Park, early 1920s. The Brudenell family of Deene owned much land in the north-east Welland Valley, and every October organized a luncheon for the tenant farmers on the estate. Here George Brudenell sits on the front row, sixth from the left.

PEACE PAGEANT AT BRAYBROOK, 1919. Some of the tableaux typical of many such events mounted throughout the Valley to celebrate the official end of World War One.

VJ DAY STREET PARTY, Walcot Road, Market Harborough, 1945. With many local servicemen involved in the campaign in the Far East, the end of the war with Japan was an especially appropriate time for a street party.

VJ DAY STREET PARTY, Walcot Road, Market Harborough, 1945. Besides the party for children, these residents of Walcot Road, produced a solidarity banner (where is it now?) and effigies of Hirohito and Hitler, which were burnt that night.

CORONATION PROCESSION, Medbourne, 1911. Once again the procession is led by the village lodge of the Foresters.

THE DUCHESS OF YORK visits Fairfield Road School, March 1941. During this morale-boosting visit at one of the low points of the war, the Duchess met many volunteer service personnel as well as local council officials.

HRH PRINCESS ELIZABETH VISITS THORPE LUBENHAM, 1949. From the 1920s to the 1970s the Royal family were frequent informal visitors to Thorpe Lubenham Hall, home of the Wernher and (later) Phillips families. Here the Princess returns from morning service accompanied by Lt Col Harold Phillips.

VILLAGE CORONATION PARTY, Arthingworth, 1953. The coronation of Queen Elizabeth was the first opportunity for post-war Britain to celebrate without an eye on the ration books. This party was held in the cowshed of Church Farm.

ACKNOWLEDGEMENTS

Books of this nature are impossible to produce without the help of a great number of people, and this volume is no exception. As explained in the Introduction, most of the photographs reproduced here have been loaned to the Harborough Museum for copying from personal collections by a host of inhabitants of the Welland Valley. It is to these people, listed below, that the greatest thanks must go.

My colleagues at the museum — staff and volunteers — have provided invaluable help in processing and documenting the ever-growing photo collection and special thanks are due to Janet Alderson-Smith, Pam Aucott, Kate Brown, John Carter, Sue Grant, Norman Davey, Derek Ingleby and Susan Stretton. Also Steve Thursfield and Catherine Lines of Leicestershire Museums' Photographic Section deserve great praise for copying a seemingly endless supply of photographs so expertly and with such speed.

Much of the information about the photographs has been culled from extensive conversations with a number of village residents, who were always so willing to share their encyclopaedic knowledge of their area. I am especially grateful to Jack Carter, Louisa Deas, John Eaton, Ted Hall, Ken Heselton, Peter Knight, Sidney Neal, George Pickering, Sheila Southwell, Barry Summers, Frank Vendy, Albert Watts, Eric and Michael Westaway and Maurice Wilford. Also I am indebted to Stephen Barker of the Market Harborough Historical Society and Jane Barrows of the Pen Lloyd Library, who read through the book in draft and offered many useful suggestions.

A number of photographs have been reproduced from originals held at the Leicestershire Record Office (pp. 40, 89, 154), Northamptonshire County Library (pp. 24, 74, 79, 152) and the Northamptonshire Record Office (pp. 67, 90) and thanks are due to their staffs, especially Robin Jenkins, Marion Arnold and Sue Groves (respectively) for putting up with so many awkward requests. Other items have been generously loaned by the Friends of Hallaton Museum, the Husbands Bosworth Historical Society, Naseby Battle and Farm Museum, and the Weston by Welland Village History Group.

Last, but by no means least, I am eternally indebted to my wife Lynne for providing so much love, care and attention to detail during the eighteen months this book has been in the making.

O. Adkins, D. Allen, R. Arnold, G. Bale, M. C. Barker, S. Barker, T. Barratt, P. Berry, J. D. Berry, G. Bevins, M. Bradley, M. Brooks, R. Brown, B. Brown, E. Bryant, J. Burton, J. Carter, E. Clipston, A. Cornwall, J. C. Davies, M. Dawkins, O. de Rousset-Hall, L. Deas, W. Falkner, J. Falkner, D. Fisher, G. Fox, P. Fox, B. Freer, G. Freeston, J. Fretter, F. Goodman, M. Goodman, V. Gray, S. Hammond, P. Higgs, K. Holland, R. Holyoak, W. Howlett, S. Johnson, N. Kavanagh, R. King, H. Law, D. Lewin, J. Little, M. Manser, R. Martin, C. Medley, M. Monk, J. Morris, P. Mottley, S. Neal, D. Odell, R. Payne, E. W. Pearson, F. J. Phillips, G. Pickering, M. Punter, R. Radia, K. Reynolds, D. Robinson, J. Sanderson, A Savage, A Seabrook, C. M. Smith, T. Smith, S. Southwell, M. Stevens, P. Stimson, K. Swingler, F. Taylor, R. Teear, L. Tibbits, C. Tozer, W. Trigg, V. Twynham, D. Verspeak, A. Watts, W. Webb, A. J. Welch, J. West, E. Westaway, M. Westaway, M. Wilford, M. Withers, M. Woodcock, G. Woolman.